A Personal Workbook

THE GOSPEL
WHAT IS IT?

Alistair Hornal

GW01418223

Partnership
Churches networking for mission

Personal workbook series aim:

To engage with the text of the Bible and develop a clear personal understanding of its central teaching. This will involve consideration of the range of alternative interpretations of the text held by Bible-believing Christians so that you can make an informed personal decision.

The authors don't attempt to hide their own views. But neither do they want to impose them on others. We want to encourage everyone to come to their own conclusions in the light of Scripture while respectfully disagreeing with those who see things differently. 'Sitting on the fence' is not a particularly comfortable position – though it may sometimes be the most sensible place to be until we have enough confidence to decide on which side we want to get off!

However, though there may be a range of legitimate interpretations (especially of finer points of biblical teaching), there is so much that God has made clear and on which we can expect to find agreement as disciples of the Lord Jesus Christ. Being open to good questions will not only make us more confident that we have rightly understood what is written in the Bible but will help us communicate Bible truth to others with gentleness and humility. (Few people appreciate the 'know all' with 'right answers'!)

The workbook series can also be used in the context of a study group or leadership team to sharpen one another's thinking and to develop a consensus view where that is needed to be effective in Christian mission.

Bible quotes are from the New International Version (2011) unless specified otherwise.

THE GOSPEL – WHAT IS IT?
A PERSONAL WORKBOOK

Contents

1. Introduction – first thoughts

The gospel – what is it?

The question seems so basic: doesn't every Christian know the gospel? (For without it, what sort of 'Christian' are you?) Yet when Paul wrote to the Christians in Galatia (probably one of the earliest New Testament documents written to a church that Paul himself had only recently planted) he was concerned that they were already 'turning to a different gospel – which is really no gospel at all' (Galatians 1:6-7). As you read through that letter, you discover that some other Christian teachers who shared Paul's Jewish heritage were now teaching these new Christians (who were not Jews) that in order to be full members of the people of God, they had to keep the Old Testament laws – starting with circumcision. There is no reason to think the new teachers had any intention to contradict the gospel Paul had preached, rather to fill it out and make the new Christians' understanding of the gospel more biblical. But Paul clearly didn't see it that way! For him, this was 'another gospel', a perversion of the gospel of Christ which was confusing these new believers. His condemnation couldn't be stronger: 'let them be under God's curse.'[1]

Adding to the gospel changes the gospel to a different gospel which is no gospel at all. That danger always remains with us. But equally, there is the danger of missing out important gospel truth – which could also result in a different gospel.

Paul's strong language shows us how serious it is to mess with this message. We need to be clear about our answer to the question: 'What is the gospel?'

In recent years, some well-intentioned Christian teachers have tended to emphasise only the love of God and play down the righteous judgment of God – simply by not talking about it. Does that make it a different gospel?

---

1   Galatians 1:8 – and to emphasise the point, he repeats the same words in verse 9.

Write down the key components of the gospel message as you understand it. (At the end of the workbook there will be an opportunity to review what you write now.) This note is 'for your eyes only'!

2. The gospel according to Jesus

The Lord Jesus didn't write any books. He could have done[2] – and we might wish he had left us a personal, definitive record of his teaching. But he didn't. Instead, we have four 'Gospels' that together enable us to build a picture of Jesus, what he said and did. These 'Gospels' were a new sort of literature, capturing forever the oral teaching of Jesus and the apostles whom Jesus had commissioned to teach what he had taught them.[3] But the word we translate as 'gospel'[4] – meaning 'good news' – was already in use.

What are the benefits of having four Gospels?

---

2   Though clearly a gifted oral teacher, Jesus was literate: he read from the Scriptures in the Nazareth synagogue (Luke 4:16-19) though we only read of him writing on the ground with his finger (John 8:6).
3   Matthew 28 :18-20
4   εὐαγγέλιον *euangelion* – from which we get 'evangel', 'evangelist', etc. See chapter 5.

What might have been the downside of only having Jesus' own record of his teaching?

_____

_____

_____

_____

_____

_____

The earliest Gospel was probably Mark.[5] It begins:

The beginning of the good news about Jesus the Messiah, the Son of God.

Mark continues in verses 14-15:

After John was put in prison, Jesus went into Galilee, proclaiming the good news of God. 'The time has come,' he said. 'The kingdom of God has come near. Repent and believe the good news!'

5 Some scholars still think that Matthew was the earliest Gospel, but most think Mark came first — and is likely to reflect the way Peter told the gospel story.

REALITY CHECK

What are the main elements of the gospel according to this earliest Gospel record?

_____

_____

_____

_____

_____

_____

_____

_____

How fully are they reflected in your personal summary of the gospel
in the 'first thoughts' section above?

_____

_____

_____

_____

_____

_____

Matthew, Mark and Luke all tell the story of Jesus along similar lines.[6] Matthew tends to make explicit a lot of things we might have to work out for ourselves if we only had Mark. One of the big lessons we discover is that Jesus didn't proclaim the whole of the gospel message all at once. Rather, it is a message in two parts: he didn't go on to the second part until his disciples had begun to grasp part 1. But it is clearly important not to lose sight of part 1 when we go on to part 2.

Before continuing with the workbook, it might be worth reading through Mark's Gospel in its entirety – preferably in a single sitting (it doesn't take long!) – and noting some of the highlights:

NOTES ON MARK

▶▶

6   That's why they are often called the 'synoptic' gospels – they come from the same viewpoint. John gives us a different and complementary perspective on Jesus.

_____

_____

_____

_____

_____

_____

_____

_____

Matthew provides us with an explicit marker for each of the two parts of Jesus' presentation of the gospel:

Part 1   Matthew 4:12-17

When Jesus heard that John had been put in prison, he withdrew to Galilee. (v. 12)

From that time on Jesus began to preach, 'Repent, for the kingdom of heaven has come near.' (v. 17)

Part 2   Matthew 16:21

From that time on Jesus began to explain to his disciples that he must go to Jerusalem and suffer … and that he must be killed and on the third day be raised to life.

Matthew 16:13-28 is, therefore, a pivotal passage,[7] marking the climax of Part 1 of the Gospel according to Jesus and the beginning of Part 2.

Look it up and note for yourself:

What had Simon discovered – by divine revelation – about who Jesus is?

Why do you think the disciples were ordered not to tell?

7   Matthew expands on Mark 8:27-30 (cf. Luke 9:18-27).

BACKGROUND NOTES

Three key terms:

1. **son of man**

   This was Jesus' favourite way of referring to himself. It is a common expression, used many times in Ezekiel to address the prophet. It simply means 'human being'; Scots might paraphrase it as 'laddie' or Welsh as 'boyo'! But on one notable occasion (Daniel 7:13-14) it refers to 'one like a son of man' who approaches the Ancient of Days and receives universal authority. Bible translations often bring this out by using capital letters: Son of Man. But Jesus was intentionally ambiguous.

Why do you think Jesus might have found this such a useful term to conceal – in full view – his identity until it was time for it to be revealed?

_____

_____

_____

_____

_____

_____

_____

_____

How does Matthew make the connection to Daniel 7:13-14 at the end of his Gospel?

Look up Matthew 28:18. What does this tell us about Jesus in light of Daniel 7:13-14?

2. **Messiah**

Messiah reflects a Hebrew term meaning 'anointed one'. Most commonly, it is a royal title, but priests were also anointed with oil. Our word 'Christ' comes from a Greek term with the same meaning.[8] While the priestly association also fits perfectly with Jesus,[9] it is the regal element that is brought clearly into focus by Jesus himself[10] leading to his execution as 'King of the Jews'.[11]

3. **The kingdom of God**[12]

It is best not to think of the kingdom of God in geographical terms (like the United Kingdom) rather in terms of God's rule or reign. (Some scholars favour God's 'kingship'.) By saying that God's reign is at hand/has come near, Jesus is effectively pointing to the fact that he is the kingdom's king!

8   John 1:41 makes this very point for his Greek speaking readers.
9   Hebrews 6:20 portrays Jesus as 'a high priest forever, in the order of Melchizedek' and the following chapter spells out the significance of seeing Jesus as a Priest-King.
10 E.g. Matthew 21:1-5; 22:41-46
11 See e.g. Matthew 27:11-37
12 Matthew uses the phrase 'kingdom of heaven' with the same meaning. Matthew's phrase reflects a common Jewish preference for indirect references to God. 'Heaven reigns' = 'God reigns'.

Part 1 of Jesus' presentation of the gospel climaxes in the declaration that this 'son of man' – in every respect human[13] - is God's anointed king.[14]

Part 2 shows how the king must be killed – and raised from death. It is the risen Christ who declares himself to have 'all authority in heaven and on earth',[15] thus bringing out the full significance of Jesus as 'Son of Man'… who is no less than the 'Son of God'.

It is only on the eve of his crucifixion that Jesus explains the significance of his death to his disciples. But he does it in the most graphic manner. You can read what he told them in **Matthew 26:17-30.**

What do you think was significant about the timing of Jesus' death?
(It is perhaps worth noting how John's Gospel reports John the Baptist's introduction of Jesus – see John 1:29 – when reading Matthew 26:17.)

---

13 Jesus was like us in every way apart from sin see e.g. Romans 8:3, Hebrews 4:15.
14 'Son of God' was also a royal designation in the Old Testament (e.g. Psalm 2:6-7). Maybe that is as much as Simon Peter had yet understood about who Jesus was at Matthew 16:16. If so, he spoke better than he knew: this king really was God's Son!
15 Matthew 28:16-20

What does Jesus bring to mind from the Old Testament by talking about 'blood of the covenant'?[16]

While Matthew and Mark report Jesus personalising the blood of the covenant as 'my' blood, Luke adds a further dimension. In Luke 22:20, the Lord Jesus speaks with a resounding echo of Jeremiah 31:31-34.

What can you discover from Jeremiah 31:31-34 about the gospel according to Jesus?

16 See Exodus 24:6-8 for the origin of the expression. Zechariah 9:9-11 shows us that Jesus was dropping big hints already about the 'blood of the covenant' by the way he approached Jerusalem on his way to the cross.

What else can you see in Jeremiah 31 that makes connections with the gospel?

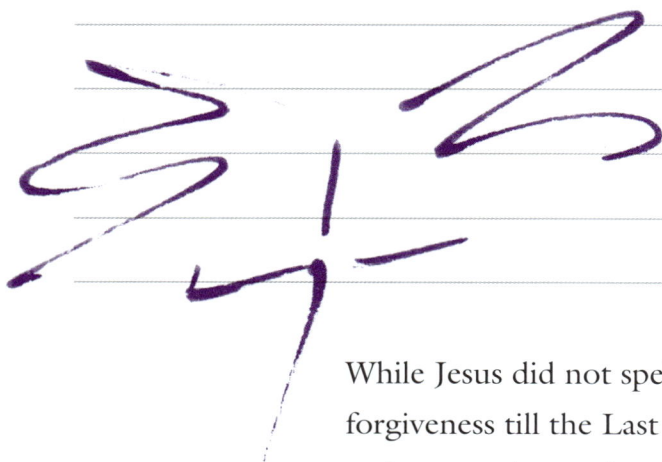

_____

_____

_____

_____

_____

_____

While Jesus did not spell out the significance of his death in terms of our forgiveness till the Last Supper, he was immediately clear to his disciples – then and now – about what it means to 'follow him'.

How would you summarise from **Matthew 16:24-28** both the cost and the benefit of following in Jesus' footsteps?

_____

_____

_____

_____

_____

_____

BACKGROUND NOTE: DISCIPLE

In the culture of Jesus' day, people who chose to learn from a particular teacher were known as his 'disciples'. While celebrities today are likely to have many 'followers' on social media, in those days disciples literally followed their master around. The best example we have today is the ward round, where students, nurses and junior medical staff follow the consultant as he instructs them about patient treatment.

Being a disciple of Jesus is not a classroom (or armchair!) exercise. It is a call to follow him – whatever the personal cost. For the outcome couldn't be better.

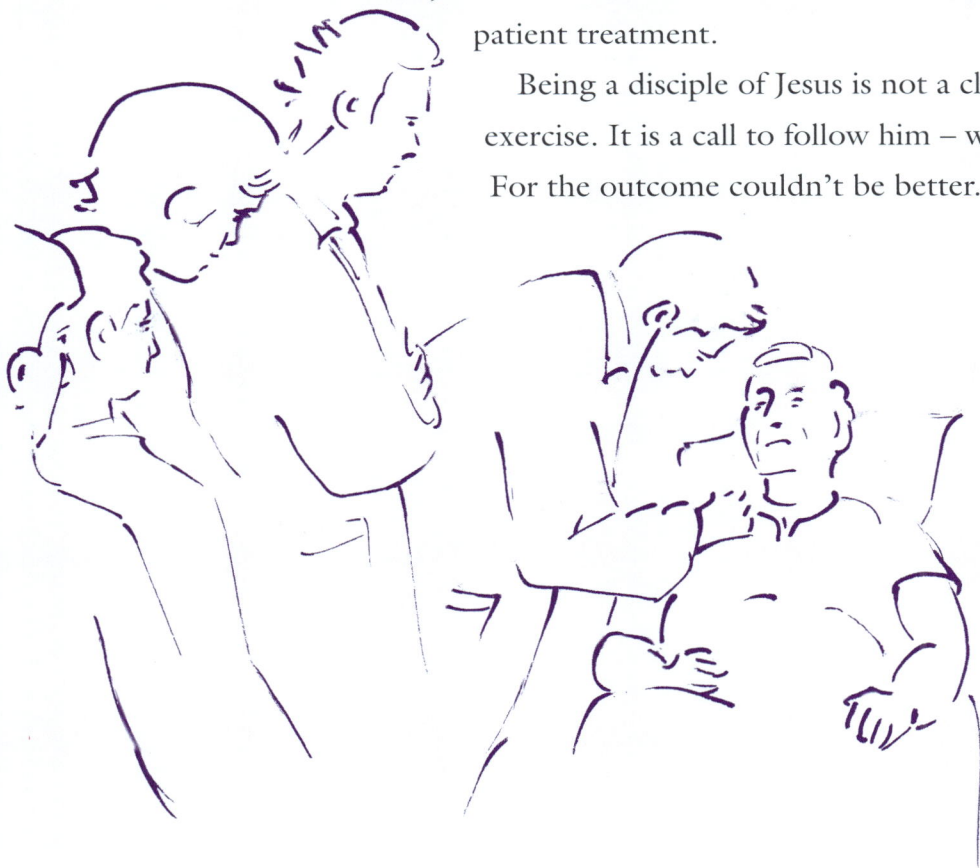

We saw that Mark opens his Gospel with:

The beginning of the good news about Jesus the Messiah, the Son of God.

It is only as we read through the Gospels that we discover just how good the 'good news' is.

Mark also records the headline of Jesus' own initial gospel message:

After John was put in prison, Jesus went into Galilee, proclaiming the good news of God. 'The time has come,' he said. 'The kingdom of God has come near. Repent and believe the good news!'[17]

There's a lot packed into that headline – as we'll discover when we look at how the apostle Paul unpacks the gospel!

17   Mark 1:14-15

3. The gospel according to Paul

In Romans 1:16-17 Paul declares:

[16] For I am not ashamed of the gospel, because it is the power of God that brings salvation to everyone who believes: first to the Jew, then to the Gentile. [17] For in the gospel the righteousness of God is revealed – a righteousness that is by faith from first to last, just as it is written: 'The righteous will live by faith.'

So, what does Paul mean by 'the gospel'?

WHAT IS 'THE GOSPEL' ACCORDING TO PAUL?

In his letter to the church at Rome (which he had never visited – but hoped to stop off there *en route* to mission work in Spain[18]) Paul provides his most comprehensive presentation of the gospel that he preached. He outlines his main themes in his opening paragraph:

Paul, a servant of Christ Jesus, called to be an apostle and set apart for the gospel of God – [2] the gospel he promised beforehand through his prophets in the Holy Scriptures [3] regarding his Son, who as to his earthly life was a descendant of David, [4] and who through the Spirit of holiness was appointed the Son of God in power by his resurrection from the dead: Jesus Christ our Lord.

ROMANS 1:1-4

---

18   Romans 15:23-24

It is worth noting the following phrases in particular:

■ **'the gospel of God'**

We have already seen Mark's use of this phrase – unique in the Gospels, but more common in Paul.[19] It could mean 'God's gospel' – good news that belongs to/comes from God; equally it could mean good news about God. Paul may have both meanings in mind!

Did this aspect of the gospel feature in your own first thoughts? P. 5

How might a focus on **God** counterbalance any tendency to think that the gospel is principally good news for me?

■ **'promised … in the Scriptures'**

There are aspects of the gospel that are new and could not be known until Jesus came. They are promised – but we don't know who they apply to. The Old Testament promises a Messiah – and points to 'one like a Son of Man'. We now know that the promised one is Jesus! That is the very heart of the Good News.

19   Mark 1:14; Romans 1:1; 15:16; 2 Corinthians 11:7; 1 Thessalonians 2:2,8,9. (See also 1 Peter 4:17.)

Most of the categories[20] in which we express the gospel are drawn from what we call the 'Old Testament' – which is the Bible that Jesus (and the New Testament writers) read, and called 'the Scriptures'. These categories relate in large part to the Old Testament sacrificial system – which was itself a sort of promise. The Old Testament sacrifices were a 'working model' that didn't actually work![21] But they demonstrate the principles on which God acts in grace and mercy towards us – and hold the promise of the Sacrifice that would eventually deliver.[22]

■ **'regarding his Son … a descendant of David'**

God's gospel is first and foremost about Jesus: as the heavenly Voice declared at Jesus' baptism[23] and transfiguration:[24] 'This is my Son'. Matthew's Gospel in particular focuses our attention on Jesus as a descendant of David,[25] pointing us clearly to the conclusion that Jesus is the promised Messiah (or 'the Christ').

■ **'appointed the Son-of-God-in-power according to the Holy Spirit by the resurrection from the dead'[26]**

While eternally in relation to the Father as Son,[27] Jesus' resurrection marks a further and unique declaration of his divine sonship – including all its regal overtones.[28]

■ **'Jesus Christ our Lord'**

Taking all of this together, it seems that at the heart of the gospel for Paul is

---

20   E.g. redemption, justification, atonement.
21   See Hebrews 10:1-4.
22   See Hebrews 10:5-10.
23   Matthew 3:17; cf. Mark 1:11, Luke 3:22 where Jesus is addressed directly: 'You are my Son'.
24   Matthew 17:5; Mark 9:7; Luke 9:35
25   Matthew's genealogy of Jesus is structured around David (Matthew 1:1-17) and the birth narratives in both Matthew and Luke reinforce the connection with David – while also making clear his uniquely divine sonship through his virgin birth.
26   NET Bible
27   And verbally owned as Son by the Father – see footnotes 23 & 24 above.
28   E.g. Psalm 2:6-7 – indeed the whole psalm.

the world-changing fact that **the promised Messiah is Jesus** – and what his kingship means. This is not only profoundly counter-cultural (to declare that 'Jesus Christ is Lord' – in Rome of all places, where no-one but Caesar is lord) but an evident echo of the gospel according to Jesus: 'The kingdom of heaven has come near. Repent and believe the good news!'[29]

That same response to the gospel is what Paul is calling the nations to; he calls it 'the obedience of faith' (Romans 1:5 taken quite literally) or perhaps 'faithful obedience'.[30]

When Paul writes, 'I am not ashamed of the gospel', he does not leave us guessing about what he means by 'the gospel'. He has already outlined its core content in his opening sentences. And if we are in any doubt about his gospel priorities, he reiterates them at the end of the letter.

What elements of Romans 1:1-7 do you see reflected in Romans 16:25-27?

_____

_____

_____

_____

_____

_____

29 Mark 1:15. While several of Paul's letters are likely to have been penned before any of the written Gospels, the content of the Gospels was part of the oral tradition of the early church – and lies behind the teaching we find in the Epistles. It is important that we read the New Testament letters as unpacking the gospel Jesus preached and embodied. This is by no means a different gospel!
30 See p. 24.

Is there anything about the gospel you had expected to see that Paul *hasn't* included in these opening and closing sections of Romans?

WHAT DOES THE GOSPEL DO?

Romans 1:16-17 is Paul's summary statement on what the gospel does.

■ **The gospel reveals God's righteousness (v. 17)**

As we have seen, Paul's gospel is very much 'the gospel of God'. It is God's revelation of his own righteousness – which is best thought of in personal and relational terms. This is important, because if we think about righteousness as primarily a legal matter, we may misunderstand Paul's argument in Romans. All God does is consistent with his character; he is himself the 'gold standard' against which all righteousness can be compared. And he always keeps his commitments. Paul demonstrates that God keeps his word: he does what is right; he will put everything right; and he will do it right.

How does the gospel reveal God's righteousness according to Romans 3:21-26?

Translating from another language is never easy as often there is not a 1:1 correspondence between words: a word in another language may carry a different range of meanings from its nearest equivalent in English. The Greek word we translate as 'faith' can also mean 'faithfulness'. See the NIV text and footnote *h* on Romans 3:22. Translators have to make a choice.[31]

The way the English language has developed means that we have a range of words, some based on 'just' (justice, justify etc.) and some based on 'right' (righteous, righteousness) to represent a single word group in Greek. Paul draws on great concepts that God has revealed in the Old Testament – sin, justification, redemption, atonement, faith – and shows how not only the Old Testament sacrifices but the stories of how God deals with his people (whether individuals like Abraham or David or the people of Israel as a whole) show the consistency of his ways. God does what he says!

Not only does the Old Testament Law spell out the way God does things right and puts things right, the Prophets reinforce and apply the same consistent message. The whole Old Testament – 'the Law and the Prophets' (Romans 3:21) – bear witness to God's right dealings with his people. This in turn gives us the framework for understanding what God has done in Jesus – and that he is quite right to put us into a right relationship with him through trusting in Jesus' faithfulness.

31 The NET Bible jumps the other way, putting in the main text 'through the faithfulness of Jesus Christ for all who believe' and offering 'faith in Christ' in the margin. NET Bible's footnote offers a characteristically helpful note on the translation: 'A decision is difficult here. Though traditionally translated "faith in Jesus Christ," an increasing number of NT scholars are arguing that … [πίστις Χριστοῦ (*pistis christou*) means] … "Christ's faith" or "Christ's faithfulness".' It then gives references to scholars on both sides of the debate.

■ The gospel is God's power that brings salvation (v. 16)

The word translated 'salvation' includes the idea of 'healing' – which is why Jesus' healing miracles are such an important pointer to what he came to do. But it means more than that, as his stories and actions make clear. (The way Jesus deals with Zacchaeus[32] is an excellent example of how 'the Son of Man came to seek and to save the lost.'[33])

It is important to recognise that 'salvation' is an effect of the gospel rather than thinking of it as the essence of the gospel. The gospel is the good news of God concerning his Son understood in the light of what God has had written in the Holy Scriptures.[34] That the gospel brings salvation for those who trust in Jesus is certainly good news for us – but that is not the centre of the gospel. Rather, in the gospel we discover that Jesus is Lord, and how he powerfully works to put everything right … including people like us who have got it so wrong!

Furthermore, God's salvation is much more than our 'get out of hell free' card. Through the gospel we discover the extent of what God has done for us in Jesus – and is doing in us as we respond to the gospel.

HOW DOES THE GOSPEL DO IT?

In one word, by 'faith'. However, as we have just seen, when we read about 'faith' we also need to think about 'faithfulness'. We use words like 'belief' and 'trust' (and the word groups that go with them) to spell out this important central concept. Whatever word the translators opt for, Bible readers need to keep the whole range of meanings in mind.

32 Luke 19:1-10
33 Luke 19:10
34 See Romans 1:1-3.

Look up a few translations of Romans 3:3 and make a note of the variations on this theme.

_____

_____

_____

_____

_____

_____

The overall message of Romans is that **God can be trusted**.

God is faithful. So, we can trust him (have 'faith' in him) – and become faithful.

We are 'put right to live right', and not just by 'keeping the Law' but by coming into a relationship of 'covenant faithfulness' with a God who keeps faith with his faithful ones – and above all with the Lord Jesus Christ, the ultimate Faithful One.

WHO IS THE GOSPEL FOR?

■ first to the Jew

Here, the apostle Paul is clearly walking in the footsteps of the Master. Jesus makes this priority (uncomfortably) clear in his conversation with a Canaanite woman in Matthew 15:24 and in his instructions to his disciples as he sends them on their first mission 'to the lost sheep of Israel'.[35] As we trace Paul's own practice through Acts, we see he always went first to the Jewish communities.[36]

Romans 9–11 is a central part of Paul's argument, in which he demonstrates through God's dealings with Israel that God can indeed be trusted – and why going 'first to the Jew' is so important (even though many Jews will resist the gospel) if the gospel is to reach all nations and bring salvation to 'all Israel'.[37] If God doesn't keep his promises to Israel, what hope is there for anyone else?

■ then to the 'Greek'

Mark refers to the Canaanite woman as a 'Greek'.[38] This often means 'Greek speaking' rather than ethnically Greek. But equally it can simply mean 'not Jew' (so NIV translates it as 'gentile'[39] – a Jewish way of referring to people from 'the nations'). We might reasonably paraphrase Paul's priorities as 'first to the Jews – then to the rest of the world'. But those are both parts of the great universal phrase to describe who the gospel is for:

■ everyone 'faithing' (see p.24)

There is one gospel for all. Jesus Christ is Lord of all. All who believe this good news – all who have faith – benefit from God's saving power … which includes the Holy Spirit's power to transform our characters so that we become faithful followers of the Lord Jesus, through union with him.

'Justification by faith alone' was one of the great gospel truths that was recovered at the Reformation. Indeed, it is what gave hope and new life to Martin Luther and is without doubt an essential part of the gospel according to

35 Matthew 10:6
36 The story of Acts climaxes with Paul actually reaching Rome. There he discovers that the Jews in Rome are no different from those that Isaiah was sent to – or that the Lord Jesus encountered. (Acts 28:25-27, cf. Isaiah 6:9-10 and Matthew 13:14-15.) As with Jesus, his attention is given to those who will listen – and that includes people from all nations (Acts 28:28).
37 Romans 11:25-26. See also Galatians 6:16.
38 Mark 7:26
39 Romans 1:16

Paul.[40] You could be forgiven for even thinking that 'justification by faith' is the gospel – and that it is the main message of Romans. But important as this great truth is, the gospel is more than justification by faith – though never less!

The late 20th century produced a number of scholars who brought a 'new perspective' on Paul.[41] It would be a mistake to think that this 'new perspective' should simply replace the 'old perspective' of the Reformers. Rather, 'new perspective' advocates have opened up fresh angles on the meaning of the terms Paul used to express the gospel and the arguments he used to demonstrate what God has done in Christ. This may lead us to question some of the ways Christians have presented the gospel. But there is no need to throw the baby out with the bathwater.[42]

How important is it to consider fresh angles on the gospel – and even to question our own understanding of the good news in light of what is actually written in the Bible?

---

40   See Galatians and Romans in particular.
41   Notably E. P. Sanders in US. James D. G. Dunn and N. T. ('Tom') Wright are the best-known British proponents of the 'new perspective'.
42   Indeed, just because scholars raise good questions we need not always agree with their answers. It is generally helpful to read books like Romans and Galatians with good questions in mind to sharpen our understanding and come to our own conclusions which will be enriched by looking afresh at God's word from another angle.

Adding to the gospel and taking away from it are equally possible routes to producing a 'different gospel'. How can we stay true to the gospel message as we find it in Scripture?

How fully do you agree with N. T. Wright's comment?

'for Paul "the gospel" is not a system of salvation, a message first and foremost about how human beings get saved. It is an announcement about Jesus, the Messiah, the Lord.'[43]

43   N. T. Wright, 'Romans' in *New Interpreter's Bible* vol. X, Nashville: Abingdon Press 2002, p. 419.

4. First importance – full effects

Now, brothers and sisters, I want to remind you of the gospel I preached to you, which you received and on which you have taken your stand. [2]By this gospel you are saved, if you hold firmly to the word I preached to you. Otherwise, you have believed in vain.

[3]For what I received I passed on to you as of first importance: that Christ died for our sins according to the Scriptures,[4]that he was buried, that he was raised on the third day according to the Scriptures …

1 CORINTHIANS 15:1-4a

FIRST IMPORTANCE

Whether these words were first penned by Paul, or more likely part of the oral traditions of the early church that he 'received' and 'passed on', 1 Corinthians 15:3-4 contains an amazingly succinct statement of primary gospel truth.

■ Christ died

The word choice is specific. True, Jesus died. But it is the stark juxtaposition that creates such impact: Christ – the Messiah, God's King – died. This was not what was expected of Messiah; he should surely be a conquering king! It wasn't just personal affection for Jesus that caused Peter's strong (and strangely ironic) reaction: 'Never, Lord!'[44] Peter had just declared Jesus to be 'the Messiah, the Son of the living God.' (Matthew 16:16) That the Christ – the Messiah – should 'suffer … and that he must be killed' (Matthew 16:21) was unthinkable. But that very fact is right up there 'as of first importance'.

44 Matthew 16:22

■ ... for our sins

Paul would later make the relationship between death and sin very clear in Romans 5:12-21 – and the seeds of the Adam/Christ typology are already evident in 1 Corinthians 15:21-22,45-49.

Both these passages are worth looking at now.

Why do people die?

In what ways are what Jesus did similar to what Adam did?

In what ways are they different?

Like all death, then, Jesus' death was related to sin. But not his own sin – for Jesus was sinless. Paul would later write to the church at Corinth: 'God made him who had no sin to be sin for us, so that in him we might become the righteousness of God.' (2 Corinthians 5:1)[45]

That is what lies behind the Baptist's introduction of Jesus: 'Look, the Lamb of God who takes away the sin of the world!' (John 1:29).

'TYPOLOGY'

In Romans 5:14 we read that Adam was a 'pattern' of the one to come. The Greek word Paul uses gives us our English word 'type'. In the days before word processors and digital publishing, letters were produced on typewriters and books were typeset. If you looked at a typeface, you saw the mirror image of the letter it would produce on the page. It was just like the letter – but different. That helps us with what Paul is saying about Adam and Jesus. What Adam did (and his effects on humanity and the rest of creation) is mirrored in what Jesus did. It's the same basic shape – but very different in its outcome.

This idea of 'typology' is important if we are to value the Old Testament patterns and shadows[46] as a way to appreciate the multiple facets of what the Lord Jesus has accomplished. The book of Hebrews (whose author is unknown) is the fullest New Testament treatment of 'typology' and should be read alongside Paul's letters.

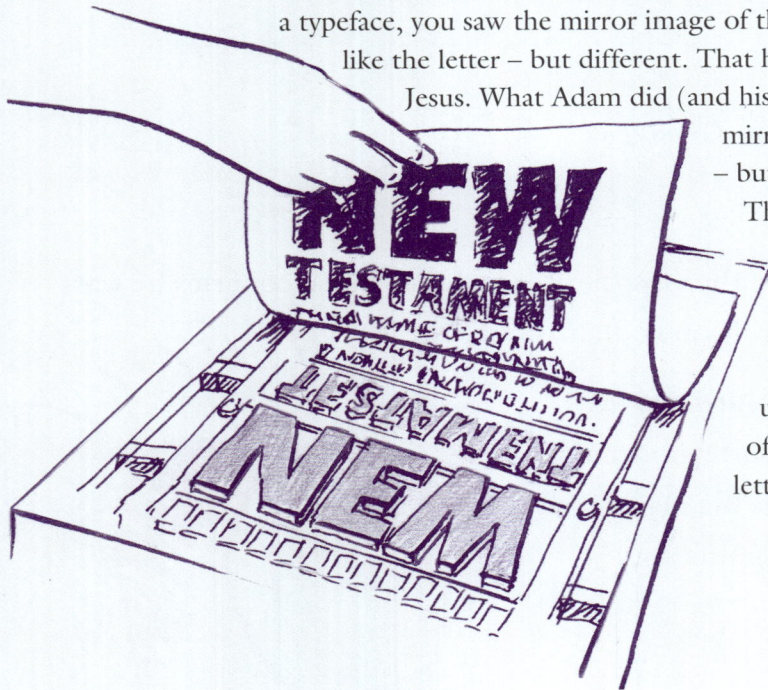

45 Cf. Romans 8:3
46 Hebrews 10:1

- **according to the Scriptures**

  To speak of death as 'for sin' is not some innovation: the very words Paul uses evoke the language of sacrifice – of the sin offering.[47]

We have already looked at Romans 3:21-26.[48] How do the Old Testament word pictures Paul refers to in that passage help us understand from the Scriptures how Jesus' death dealt with our sins?

_____

_____

_____

_____

_____

- **he was buried**

  Pointing us principally to the Gospel records, Jesus' burial confirms he was dead and prepares us for the next dramatic phrase:

- **he was raised on the third day**

  It is the fact of Jesus' resurrection and its implications for us that is the main focus of what Paul writes in 1 Corinthians 15.

---

47 Hence the NIV text of Romans 8:3 (the NIV footnote provides the literal translation); in 2 Corinthians 5:21, the sacrificial element is brought out in the footnote.
48 Pp. 23-24

How does Paul demonstrate that the resurrection was a historical fact
in 1 Corinthians 15:5-8?

What are the implications for us that he draws from Jesus' resurrection in the
rest of the chapter?

■ according to the Scriptures...

We have seen from the opening verses of Romans how Paul understands the
significance of Jesus' resurrection and how he demonstrates this from the
Scriptures.[49]

It is perhaps a bit more tricky to work out *from the Scriptures* the significance

49   Pp. 19-21

of it being on the third day. It clearly was something that Jesus repeated,[50] so it must be important.[51] And Jesus clearly points us in the right direction at Matthew 12:39-41.[52]

Does the idea of typology[53] help us understand what Jesus is saying here?

In what ways was the 'sign' like the event it signified?

How was it different?

---

50   Matthew 16:21; 17:23; 20:19
51   Is this perhaps one of the indicators that Jesus was the promised prophet like Moses? See Deuteronomy 18:18-22.
52   Interestingly, even before Jesus openly taught about his death, Matthew says he pointed to his resurrection.
53   P. 32

What other Old Testament Scriptures point to the fact or significance of Jesus' resurrection on the third day? (It's ok to use a concordance or the search function in a Bible app!)

Without doubt, this is the climax of the Good News: Christ is risen! But the gospel doesn't end there.

FULL EFFECTS

Paul goes on to report the impact of Jesus' resurrection on the apostles, referring to events that would later be recorded in the Gospels as well as an appearance to over five hundred people of which we have no other record – but would have been possible to check out at that time.[54]

That 'he appeared' is in itself evidence that there is good news to preach. Indeed, the validity of the gospel message depends on the resurrection as fact: if this is not true, the 'gospel' is so much hot air and worse than useless.[55]

'But Christ has indeed been raised from the dead' – and that is just the beginning!

Have a look at 1 Corinthians 15:20-28.
If Christ's resurrection is the 'firstfruits' what is the full harvest?

Paul uses the same phrase he applies to God – that he may be 'all in all'[56] – but he applies it to Christ in Ephesians 1:23.[57]

54   1 Corinthians 15:5-8
55   See Paul's own graphic statements in 1 Corinthians 15:12-19.
56   1 Corinthians 15:28
57   NIV translates it as 'everything in every way', but the words are the same in Greek. (Colossians 3:11 is similar.)

Compare and contrast what Paul writes in Ephesians 1 with what you have read in 1 Corinthians 15.

_____

_____

_____

_____

_____

_____

How would you summarise the full effects of the gospel?

_____

_____

_____

_____

_____

_____

Ephesians 1 makes it clear that this was God's masterplan from the beginning. But it had remained a mystery till Christ appeared. Now the 'mystery' has been made known.

What light does Ephesians 1 shed on:

• The gospel according to Jesus (Matthew 4:17; 16:21)?

• What Paul wrote about 'the gospel of God' in Romans 1:1-4?

When Paul writes about 'mystery' he doesn't mean something mysterious –
rather, something that had been a puzzle has now been made known.
What else does Paul tell us about what he had discovered about this mystery …
made known in Ephesians 3:2-13?

And there's more to come!

We saw that 'salvation' is much more than a 'get out of hell free card' – and that the word translated 'salvation' carries with it the idea of bodily healing. How does the climax of Paul's gospel in Romans 8 bring this all together?

You may like to reflect on Romans 8:22-24 as you consider the 'full effects' of the gospel.

We may not be there yet, but we are very much on the way!

God has chosen
to make known among the Gentiles
the glorious riches of this mystery,
which is
Christ in you, the hope of glory.[58]

COLOSSIANS 1:27

58 Cf. Ephesians 3:6

REVIEW PAGE

Before we continue with the next chapter, take a few minutes to think about:

What is 'new' about the Good News?

_____

_____

_____

_____

_____

What elements of the gospel do we find in the Old Testament?

_____

_____

_____

_____

_____

_____

_____

5. Roots and Shoots

A. CULTURAL ROOTS

When the apostle Paul proposed to preach this 'gospel' in Rome of all places (see Romans 1:7) it was bound to make an impact.

Rome was the superpower of the day – the centre of a huge empire surrounding the Mediterranean and stretching from Spain to Babylonia (modern Iraq), from Britain to Egypt. Subduing and ruling such an extensive and diverse population not only involved a fair degree of diplomacy but a significant amount of syncretism, incorporating many diverse religions.

Rome itself was a centre of Emperor worship. The Caesars had taken to the practice of deifying their predecessors so they could themselves be considered to be a 'Son of God.' Caesars were known as 'saviours' and major events in their lives were announced as 'good news' – using the same word we translate as 'gospel.'

So, to ask people to declare allegiance to Jesus as Lord (where any loyal Roman would declare, 'Caesar is Lord') was bound to be an attention-grabber. And that is just what Paul was asking Christians in Rome to do:

> if you declare with your mouth,
> 'Jesus is Lord,'
> and believe in your heart that God
> raised him from the dead,
> you will be saved.
>
> ROMANS 10:9

The Christian gospel – that Jesus is Messiah, God's anointed king – was a direct challenge to imperial power and to the emperor cult that sustained it.

Contemporary impact was guaranteed!

...RUNNING DEEP INTO HISTORY

Of course, Rome was only the last in a line of empires which had swallowed up the land that God had promised to his people, Israel. In the ancient world, conquest was not just viewed in military terms but as a battle of gods – with the defeated gods being drawn under the power of the gods of the victorious army. Isaiah 37:10-13 records a typical expression of this.

The central section of Isaiah (chapters 36–39) provides us with the historical context for a prophetic ministry that had been launched with a vision of the glory of God who lives and reigns when human kings die. (See Isaiah 6:1 ff.)

But God's people did not listen to Isaiah's 'bad' news; so, God had not only allowed his people to be conquered by the Assyrians – who exerted their power by moving whole people groups to new locations around their empire – but he would later overrule through the rise of the Persian empire to bring about a return from Exile.

If Assyria is the instrument of God's judgment in the earlier part of Isaiah (see Isaiah 10:5-19), God also promises he will preserve a 'remnant' of his people and bring them back from Exile (Isaiah 10:20 ff.) – with the promise of a new king: a fresh 'shoot' from the cut-down 'stump' of David's dynasty, the 'root' of Jesse (Isaiah 11:1).

The promised return from Exile provides the context for the 'good news' prophecies in the second part of this major book which bears Isaiah's name, and which is often (rightly!) seen as the grandest statement of the gospel in the Old Testament.

B. THE GOSPEL: OLD TESTAMENT ROOTS

The word translated 'good news' in the Greek translation of the Old Testament is from the same word group that is represented by 'gospel' in the New Testament: εὐαγγέλιον (euangelion). It is the word from which we get English words like 'evangelist' and 'evangelical'. The prefix 'eu' means 'good' – so, for example, 'euthanasia' adds it to the Greek word for death, so literally 'a good death'. You can also see our word 'angel' in euangelion. Angels are messengers – 'newscasters' if you like. 'Good news' is a pretty good translation, therefore. And the scholars who translated Isaiah's Hebrew text into Greek used its verbal form: those who bring good news to Zion (see Isaiah 40:9; 52:7) are quite literally 'evangelising'!

The translators have chosen this verb to represent Isaiah's original Hebrew root: bāśar.

The Christian gospel was framed in language that was evidently relevant to the prevailing culture, but it was not shaped by that culture. It sprang from deeper roots. Judea and Palestine were part of the Roman empire – and even Jewish religious leaders who would have balked at the idea of worshipping the Emperor had no qualms about declaring: 'We have no king but Caesar' (John 19:15). In their desire to be rid of this nuisance who kept challenging their traditions (and their authority) had they forgotten the grand theme of their Scriptures (what we call the 'Old Testament') that the LORD reigns – that Yahweh is King?

How beautiful on the mountains
    are the feet of those who bring good news,
who proclaim peace,
    who bring good tidings,
    who proclaim salvation,
who say to Zion,
    'Your God reigns!' ISAIAH 52:7

Isaiah pictures a herald running with good news[59] to Jerusalem. The main message of the first part of Isaiah[60] is not such good news – at least, not in the short term. God's people will be sent into exile. There is a 'stay of execution' in the days of King Hezekiah, the story that provides the historical hub of the

---

59   It is his good news that makes even the *feet* of the messenger seem beautiful (Isaiah 52:7).
60   Isaiah 1–35

book.[61] But then the second part of Isaiah[62] looks beyond the exile to a period of restoration. It is this message of hope – of a return from exile brought about by God's sovereign hand – that is the 'salvation' that is in mind. Peace and well-being – *shalom* – come as a result of God's reign over human affairs.

It is the same principle at work in the gospel according to Paul: God's power that brings salvation.[63] It is the same good news that Jesus preached: God's kingdom had come near.[64] But the gospel according to Isaiah points beyond the return from Exile to even better 'good news' – to a conquering heavenly king[65] and the creation of new heavens and a new earth[66] that echoes the earlier vision of Isaiah 2:1-5.[67] Isaiah's words are re-echoed and amplified at the end of Revelation,[68] and remain part of our Christian hope. But the second half of Isaiah also introduces us to the one through whom this salvation comes.

THE GOSPEL IN THE OLD TESTAMENT

■ **Isaiah 40**

The second major prophetic section of Isaiah rings out with a message of comfort as divine tenderness is given prophetic voice.

---

61 Isaiah 36–39; cf. 2 Kings 18–20
62 Often called 'Second Isaiah' (or 'Deutero-Isaiah') and thought by most Old Testament scholars to come from a later era and a different author than the first part. However, there is a body of evangelical scholarship that argues for the unity of the book as a pre-exilic composition (e.g. Alec Motyer, The Prophecy of Isaiah, IVP Leicester, 1993) and it is unlikely that Jesus would have thought of it other than as a unified composition.
63 Romans 1:16
64 Mark 1:15
65 Isaiah 63:1-6,15; 66:1
66 Isaiah 65:17
67 Cf. Micah 4:1-5
68 Revelation 21–22

What can you discover about God's gentle use of power in the face of human frailty and failings from Isaiah 40:1-11?

How is this prophetic message picked up in Matthew 3?

In Matthew 4 the herald makes way for the kingdom's King. How does Matthew skilfully point us back to Isaiah's Good News message?

One of the distinctive features of Matthew's Gospel is the way he refers to the Old Testament. On ten occasions he uses a formula beginning something like: 'this was to fulfil…' (Matthew 1:22-23; 2:15,17-18,23; 4:14-16; 8:17; 12:17-21; 13:35; 21:4-5; 27:9-10.)

When you look up each of these formula quotations, though, you discover that Matthew is not just providing a set of predictions that we can simply use as prophetic proof texts pointing to Jesus. (If we try to do that, any careful reader of the Old Testament text will rightly question our credibility.) Rather, as Matthew reflects on the events of Jesus' life and ministry, he sees clear connections with what is written in the Old Testament. And when you read the selected quotations in their original setting you discover that they function like keys which open up a treasure chest of insights about Jesus.

Not only do they shed an immense amount of light on what Jesus came to do, but in Jesus there is even more than the Old Testament writer might have had in mind. That's what Matthew means by 'fulfil': Jesus fills the Old Testament full!

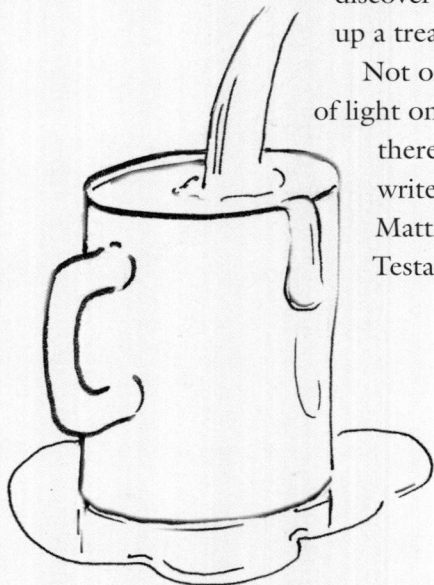

A good case can be made to show that it was Jesus himself who taught his disciples to read the Old Testament in this way.

For example, Matthew records Jesus speaking about fulfilment on three significant occasions (Matthew 5:17; 13:14; 26:54,56).

Luke not only records how the risen Christ said to his disciples,

> 'This is what I told you while I was still with you: everything must be fulfilled that is written about me in the Law of Moses, the Prophets and the Psalms.' (Luke 24:44)

he also highlights Jesus' self-awareness of his mission on the eve of his crucifixion:

> 'It is written: "And he was numbered with the transgressors"; and I tell you that this must be fulfilled in me. Yes, what is written about me is reaching its fulfilment.' (Luke 22:37)

Jesus not only knew what was about to happen, he made the explicit link with the Old Testament by quoting Isaiah 53:12. Matthew similarly points us to the same chapter with one of his formula quotations. This section of Isaiah was evidently in regular use by the early Christian preachers – perhaps most notably as Philip starts from this very passage which the Ethiopian eunuch just 'happened' to be reading and tells him the good news about Jesus. (Acts 8:32-35)

Isaiah 52:13–53:12 is one of a series of poems which feature God's servant – a figure who dominates Isaiah 40–55. These poems are often called the Servant Songs.

In Acts 8:26-40, Philip the evangelist was sent to speak to an Ethiopian official who was reading Isaiah as he travelled home from Jerusalem. He had got as far as Isaiah 53 when Philip joined him, but clearly was not understanding what he was reading (Acts 8:30-31).

What do you make of the Ethiopian official's question (verse 34)?

What do you think Philip would have pointed out in Isaiah 52:13–53:12 to tell this man 'the good news about Jesus'?

The Servant in the second part of Isaiah is undoubtedly good news, and his work prepares us for the revelation of the full consequences of his achievement in the new universe. This doesn't just 'happen' in some impersonal way, however. The closing chapters of Isaiah introduce us to a figure Alec Motyer aptly designates as Anointed Conqueror. So, who is this?

As you read Isaiah 63:1-6, who do you think this is?

What elements of Isaiah's description can you see reflected in John's revelation of Jesus[69] in Revelation 19:11-16?

---

69   John explicitly tells us that he is showing us 'a revelation of Jesus Christ' (Revelation 1:1 translated literally). Jesus is the key to unlocking Revelation's mysteries – as indeed it is Jesus who brings all that God has revealed in Scripture into clearest focus.

Just judgment and salvation are two sides of the same coin.

Isaiah speaks of the 'day of vengeance' and 'the year' to redeem (Isaiah 63:4). He uses this 'day' and 'year' language in 61:1-3 – which Jesus read in the synagogue in Nazareth (Luke 4:16-21) and began to teach by saying, 'Today this scripture is fulfilled in your hearing.'

Why do you think Jesus stopped his reading where he did?

What was being fulfilled there and then?
What part of Isaiah's prophecy would need to wait?

Reading the Bible in this way is clearly what Jesus intends his followers to do. This is how he taught. This is how the New Testament writers handle the Old Testament. All that is written in Scripture finds its true focus in Jesus. As we start with him, the whole Bible becomes 'good news'.

Similarly, the first part of Isaiah is not all 'bad news'; far from it!

EMBODYING THE MESSAGE

Isaiah is not unique in having children with significant names. Hosea also has children whose names are part of the message (Hosea 1). Indeed, Hosea (a variant of Joshua, 'Yahweh saves') has to live out with his unfaithful wife – and her illegitimate children – God's relationship with unfaithful Israel.

In Hosea's case, it is not just that the names state the message. He himself is the message lived out.

This prepares the way for Jesus (also a variant of Joshua) who not only brings the message but lives the message: Yahweh saves. He is the Word made flesh (see John 1:14). And his name says it all:

> 'you are to give him the name Jesus, because he will save his people from their sins.' (Matthew 1:21)

In Isaiah 7–8 we are introduced to Isaiah and his children who have strange but significant names; names which encapsulate Isaiah's prophetic message. Son number one, Shear-Jashub, meaning 'a remnant will return', embodies the message of the first part of the book: unless God's people repent, they will be taken into exile; yet there is hope, for 'a remnant will return'. Son number two has even more of a mouthful for a name: Maher-Shalal-Hash-Baz. But whenever his mum called him in for his tea, she was declaring the message that the Assyrians were going to make short work of carrying the Northern tribes into exile: 'quick pickings, speedy spoil'. Indeed, Isaiah's own name encapsulates his message: 'Yahweh is salvation'. Lest we be in any doubt, he tells us:

Here am I, and the children the LORD has given me. We are signs and symbols in Israel from the LORD Almighty. (ISAIAH 8:18)

It is in this context of children with significant names that we are told about a child who would carry the name 'Immanuel', meaning 'God with us'. At the time Isaiah was speaking, the young woman who would give him birth was still perhaps unmarried; but before he was old enough to know right from wrong the military threat on their doorstep would already be history. (See Isaiah 7:13-17.)

Clearly this was a sign for that time: good news for a threatened nation – if only they would listen. But Isaiah points beyond that immediate threat to the end of all war through a child who would reign forever on David's throne (Isaiah 9:1-7).

What do you think someone who had this background of Old Testament prophecy would have made of the discovery that the preacher in Galilee was the son of a young woman who actually was a virgin?

Check out Matthew 4:12-17 and Matthew 1:22-23. What do you discover?

How does this Old Testament background of significant names that encapsulate the prophet's message add to your appreciation of the name 'Jesus'? (Matthew 1:20-21)

Isaiah helps us to appreciate his message with this very personal focus. But we are still left with the insightful question posed by the Ethiopian eunuch:

'Who is the prophet talking about, himself or someone else?' ACTS 8:34

If we only had the Old Testament, it would remain an open question – and one which contains all sorts of interesting possibilities for the scholar. But once Jesus comes into view, the whole Old Testament (and Isaiah in particular) is seen in a whole new light. This is what God has done through his Servant, Jesus.

Of course, Isaiah's message doesn't stop with Jesus.

Take a look at how Peter applies Isaiah 53 in 1 Peter 2:21-25.

_____

_____

_____

_____

_____

_____

This message is not just to be believed – but lived!
(You can read Paul's take on this in 2 Corinthians 3:2-3.)

Jesus means that his followers should actually walk in his footsteps … in the way of the cross (Matthew 16:24).

6. Responding to the gospel

When we read afresh the accounts of the preaching of the apostles in Acts, it is not surprising that the gospel they preach is in full accord with the gospel according to Paul, reflecting the gospel according to Jesus.

In his famous Pentecost sermon, Peter starts with the event that is staring them in the eye: the outpouring of the Spirit – the sound like a strong wind and sight of tongues of fire on the speakers' heads – as each one heard *in their own language* about the wonders of God.[71] He makes the connection with Joel's prophecy,[72] saying 'This is *that*!'

But then he tells them about Jesus: what he had done,[73] what they had done to him,[74] but above all what God had done. Peter demonstrates that their killing of Jesus was all in the divine plan, for God's plan – made plain in the Scriptures – involved raising Jesus from death.[75] Furthermore, this is the way God would keep his promise to David that one of his descendants would reign forever.[76] And to back it up, Peter cites David's own writings in the Psalms.[77] The conclusion:

'God has made this Jesus, whom you crucified, both Lord and Messiah.'

Good news! That is the gospel.

Whenever the New Testament quotes the Old, it is worth looking it up to learn from the original context (which is often enlightening) – and to spot the differences!

Luke's record of Peter's quote from Joel actually begins with words taken from Isaiah 2:2. New Testament writers often use this device to put two Old Testament Scriptures in our mind so that we can benefit from their joint teaching.[70]

Can you spot any other differences between Peter's quote and Joel's original?

What do you think may be behind them?

---

70 The message of Isaiah 2:2-5 is very like Micah 4:1-5 – which begins with 'And'. Could Luke intend us to look up all three passages?

71 Acts 2:1-13
72 Joel 2:28-32
73 Acts 2:22
74 I.e. the 'fellow Jews and inhabitants of Jerusalem' whom he is addressing (2:14) with the help of the Romans (the 'wicked men' of 2:23).
75 Acts 2:23-28
76 2 Samuel 7:12-13
77 Psalm 16:8-11; 110:1

The reality dawns: what a dreadful mistake they had made![78] So, what can they do? Peter tells them: 'Repent and be baptised, every one of you, in the name of Jesus Christ for the forgiveness of your sins.' (Acts 2:38)

■ Repent

It's the same word Jesus used to call for a response to the good news that God's rule had come near.[79] It means more than 'feeling sorry'. It points to a complete change of mindset.[80] We might spell it out: 'You've got it so wrong! So, change the way you think – and change the way you live.'

Jesus uses the word in a general way. Peter is quite specific: 'You've got it so wrong *about Jesus*.' But when we see that and respond appropriately, there is forgiveness for all our sins.

■ Be baptised in the name of Jesus

This is a clear call for initial action. It is no 'added extra'. Baptism was counter-cultural for Jews. It was part of the initiation for non-Jews who wanted to become Jews. So, John the Baptist's invitation to Jews to be baptised was quite revolutionary.[81] It involved confessing sins[82] and was intended to lead to a new lifestyle.[83] Jesus clearly carried on baptising like John.[84] Christian baptism from Pentecost onwards continues in the same vein – but with the added twist: it is 'in the name of Jesus'. It is directly aligning with HIM.[85]

The response to the gospel that Jesus called for was:

78 Cf. Acts 3:15 'You killed the author of life, but God raised him from the dead.' These early gospel sermons are all consistent in their priority content. See also Acts 4:10-12.
79 Mark 1:15
80 μετανοέω *metanoeō* – the Greek word translated 'repent' – contains the core ideas of 'change' and 'mind'. It might well be translated 'turn'. We need to make a U-turn in our thinking about Jesus, so we see him as God does. 'Repentance' and 'faith' are therefore like two sides of the same coin: we turn from our way of thinking to trust what God says about Jesus.
81 Matthew 3:1-12
82 Matthew 3:6
83 Matthew 3:8
84 John 4:1
85 Paul amplifies in Romans 6.

'Repent and believe the good news.' MARK 1:15

Peter calls for nothing less. But believing the good news is not just something internal. It involves a complete change of mindset that acknowledges Jesus as Lord and leads to a whole new way of living: forgiven, free and following Jesus. Baptism provides the means whereby we confess with our mouth that Jesus is Lord – reflecting our belief that God has raised him from the dead.[86]

- ### Make disciples

When Jesus' disciples were baptising in Judea, this was directly linked to Jesus making disciples – and in greater numbers than John.[87] Baptism was (quite literally) a watershed: from here on, these people were committed to following Jesus. Matthew's Gospel climaxes with Jesus' instruction to the 'eleven disciples'[88] to 'make disciples'[89] of all nations. It was these disciples who were to be baptised and taught to obey all that Jesus had commanded them. In other words, the response to the gospel that Jesus is looking for is not only to say that Jesus is Lord, but to submit to his lordship by doing what he says; it is not only to believe he is God's anointed king because he has been raised from death, but to go on learning what that means by daily walking in the footsteps of Jesus.

Jesus does not hide the costliness of following him: he describes it in terms of daily taking up our cross.[90] And this is the norm for anyone who follows him – not some optional extra for super-saints. Paul reflects this in his appeal to

86   Romans 10:9
87   John 4:1-2
88   I.e. the Twelve minus Judas. See Matthew 28:16.
89   Matthew 28:19
90   Matthew 16:24

present our bodies as sacrifices – living, holy and pleasing to God.[91] And rather than carrying on in conformity to the norms of this age, we are told to be 'transformed by the renewing of our minds'[92] so that we will prove in practice the goodness and pleasing perfection of God's will. He does not use the same words;[93] but clearly, he means the same thing. The appropriate response to the gospel, an awareness of God's multiple mercies,[94] is total. (It is certainly not simply cerebral – like believing some facts about Jesus.)

■ **'By faith alone'**

Martin Luther's commentary on Galatians was particularly influential. But his interpretation of Galatians has been brought into question by the work of 'New Perspective'[95] scholars who, rather than seeing a simple 'faith versus works' contrast, read Galatians as asserting that salvation by faith in Christ[96] is sufficient without any need to be supplemented by works of the law.[97]

Ephesians 2:8-9 is more general perhaps:[98]

For it is by grace you have been saved, through faith – and this is not from yourselves, it is the gift of God – not by works, so that no one can boast.

That there can be no ground for boasting in DIY righteousness is evident from the opening verses of the chapter. We are all (Jew and Gentile alike) dependent on

91 Romans 12:1
92 Romans 12:2
93 Though μεταμορφόω *metamorphoō* by renewing of our νοός *noos* is pretty close to μετανοέω *metanoeō*!
94 See Romans 12:1.
95 See note p. 28.
96 Or even 'the faith of Christ' or 'Christ's faithfulness'. See R.B. Hays, *The Faith of Jesus Christ*, Eerdmans Grand Rapids, 2002.
97 While there is legitimate debate over the exact timing of what is recorded in Galatians 2 with regard to the Acts narrative, the issue is the one resolved in Acts 15. Its focus was circumcision (essentially, was it necessary to be circumcised to be saved?) but relates more widely to observance of the Old Testament Law.
98 Though the Jew/Gentile division, as marked by circumcision, is the focus of attention in 2:11 ff.

God's love, mercy and grace.[99] But it doesn't follow that what we do doesn't matter. Repentance and faith are two sides of the same coin.

For we are God's handiwork, created in Christ Jesus to do good works, which God prepared in advance for us to do. EPHESIANS 2:10

Good works flow from saving grace; they are the fruit of a transformed life, a necessary response to the gospel.

As we have seen, we cannot talk about faith without also thinking about faithfulness. Salvation is by faith alone – no additional 'works of the law' are necessary and it is not something we can do for ourselves – though saving faith is never alone.

This is a main feature of the message of James (famously branded an 'epistle of straw' by Luther – which possibly goes to show that even Luther cannot be the last word on this subject!) and clearly reflects the teaching of the Lord Jesus.[100] This is the response to the gospel that he is looking for.

John the Baptist called for 'fruit in keeping with repentance'[101] and his warning that 'every tree that does not produce good fruit will be cut down and thrown into the fire'[102] is echoed in Jesus' teaching about good for nothing vine branches that bear no fruit.[103] Galatians 5:22-23 describe the fruit the Spirit produces (in contrast to the works of flesh);[104] that it is fruit is a clear sign of the Spirit's work.[105] Nevertheless, we have a clear responsibility to produce it, not as a means of salvation but as a response to the gospel.

99 See Ephesians 2:4-5.
100 See e.g. the conclusion of the Sermon on the Mount (Matthew 7 :15 ff.).
101 Matthew 3:8
102 Matthew 3:10
103 John 15:6
104 Galatians 5:19-21
105 Compare John 15:4. We can only bear fruit if we remain in the true vine – Jesus.

7. Proclaiming the gospel today

For I am not ashamed of the gospel, because it is the power of God that brings salvation to everyone who believes: first to the Jew, then to the Gentile.

ROMANS 1:16

When Paul writes 'I am not ashamed', it is a subtle way of saying he is actually the very opposite of being ashamed; the gospel is what he glories in – indeed, what he goes on and on about. This is his passion; his number one priority.

As a snapshot of how Paul worked out his gospel mission strategy, we shall look at Acts 17. We shall observe the different approaches he takes in different contexts and draw out some principles to guide us in preaching the gospel in the contexts we face today.

■ first to the Jew

Acts 17 begins with Paul and his missionary colleagues in Thessalonica. As was his regular practice, he prioritises engagement with the Jewish community. (Was it because there was a synagogue in Thessalonica that Paul simply 'passed through' other places to come there?)[106] It's worth noting what Luke tells us about his methodology.

he reasoned with them from the Scriptures

The Scriptures (what Christians now regularly call the Old Testament) are the start point for his discussions. Paul was not preaching some new religion; rather – and in line with all the New Testament writers – it was his conviction

106 Acts 17:1

that the gospel was the fulfilment of the Old Testament Scriptures. Indeed, he uses categories drawn from the Old Testament[107] to explain the outworking of the gospel as God's way of salvation for everyone who believes – Jew or not. But Luke draws our attention explicitly to *what* Paul 'reasoned … from the Scriptures'.

explaining and proving that the Messiah had to suffer and rise from the dead

A suffering Messiah was not part of Jewish expectation. A conquering king, for sure. But no Jew thought that dying was a necessary part of the job description for 'Messiah'. Paul, however, carefully demonstrated from the Scriptures that suffering, death and resurrection were all part of the divine person specification. We don't know exactly which Scriptures he used – any more than we know the precise passages the Lord Jesus himself referred to on the Emmaus Road to demonstrate that 'the Messiah had to suffer these things and then enter his glory.'[108] But following Jesus' example, there were plenty to choose from![109] 'We can be reasonably sure that the Scriptures used would include Psalms 2, 16, 110; Isaiah 53; and possibly Deuteronomy 21:23.'[110]

What is important, however, is to notice Paul's methodology in this Jewish context: from the Scriptures they treasured, he demonstrated that the Messiah had to suffer and rise from the dead. Jesus alone had done this, so he must be the Messiah.

107 E.g. justification, faith(fulness), grace, redemption, atonement (Romans 3:21-26 and see p. 23ff).
108 Luke 24:26
109 'And beginning with *Moses and all the prophets*, he explained to them what was said in *all the Scriptures* concerning himself.' (Luke 24:27, emphasis added); Cf. Luke 24:44-47.
110 I. H. Marshall, *Acts*, Tyndale New Testament Commentary, Leicester: IVP 1980, p. 277

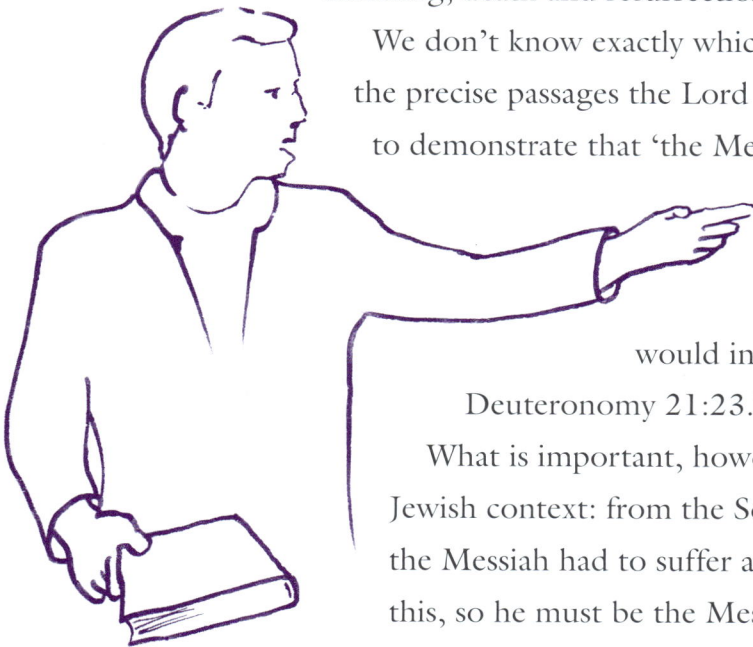

'This Jesus I am proclaiming to you is the Messiah,' he said.

The response to the gospel (i.e. that Jesus is the Messiah) among the Jewish community at Thessalonica was, at best, mixed. Some Jews were persuaded, along with 'a large number of God-fearing Greeks[111] and quite a few prominent women.' But Jewish opposition forced Paul to leave Thessalonica. He had a more favourable reception at Berea, where the Jews 'received the message with great eagerness' – though not without thoroughly checking it out: they 'examined the Scriptures every day to see if what Paul said was true.' (Acts 17:11) In consequence, many believed, Jews and Greeks, men and women.[112]

What Old Testament Scriptures would you use to demonstrate to someone who accepts the authority of the Bible that Jesus is the Messiah?

111 Many synagogues had non-Jews in attendance, serious about what the Scriptures teach about God, but without accepting the full implications of the covenant – notably circumcision.
112 Acts 17:12

How well would your case stand up to scrutiny by a serious Bible student?

Find a friend and test it out!

■ **then to the Greek**

In Athens, Paul faces a similar situation, reasoning in the synagogue (presumably on the Sabbath)[113] with both Jews and God-fearers. Day by day, though, he could be found in the marketplace, engaging in debate with local thinkers. This was new territory for them. 'Jesus and Anastasis'[114] maybe sounded to them like a pair of new gods. But we can be in no doubt that Paul's core message had not changed in this very different context. He preached the same gospel: 'Jesus and the resurrection'. What changes, though, is the basis of his reasoning.

113 Cf. Acts 17:2.
114 Acts 17:18; ἀνάστασις *anastasis* is the Greek word for 'resurrection'.

What are the key elements of Paul's argument in Acts 17:22-31?

_____

_____

_____

_____

_____

_____

How does his method change when speaking to people with no biblical background?

_____

_____

_____

_____

What doesn't change in his message?

_____

_____

_____

_____

What would be your start points to make a similar case where you live today?

How would you ensure that you don't change the message, even if you have to present it in a different way in a very different context?

Paul's message is, as ever, the gospel of God. Starting with their current realities of what they thought they knew – and knew they didn't know – about God, Paul tells them about God as creator, provider and ruler of everything. He makes it very clear that 'the Lord of heaven and earth' is no man-made god, nor does he live in man-made temples – and yet that he remains accessible. He supplies the information (which had been available all along through the Scriptures) to remove their ignorance – which God had graciously overlooked. But now Paul issues the divine command to everyone everywhere to *repent*:[115] to change the way they think – about God in particular.[116] Ignorance was no longer any excuse because something had happened to change the situation forever: by raising Jesus from the dead, God had given a clear demonstration to the whole world that a day of just judgment was now fixed – and that God's appointed judge is Jesus.

115 See pp. 54-57.
116 That is clearly what Paul means from what Luke records. When we change the way we think about God, that inevitably changes the way we live. But repentance is not primarily about moral reformation. It is principally about changing our mindset about God.

DIGGING DEEPER

Jewish opposition had forced Paul to leave Thessalonica – resulting in his letters. So, although 'Satan hindered' at that time, we get the benefit. You may find it helpful to dig beneath the surface of what we read in Acts to see what Paul would have preached at Thessalonica.

What are the main gospel themes you can see in 1 Thessalonians?

How prominent are these themes in evangelism today?

Which of them feature in the last few evangelistic talks you heard – or gave?

_____

_____

_____

_____

_____

How can we ensure people today hear the gospel of God?

_____

_____

_____

_____

_____

_____

_____

_____

_____

8. Unashamed

Without even a shadow of a doubt, Paul was 'not ashamed' of the gospel.[117] Why should he be? The gospel is good news about God. (As Paul writes later in Romans 8:31: 'If God is for us, who can be against us?') It is good news from God about his son, Jesus – raised from death, reigning as Lord. It is good news for us, because the gospel 'is the power of God that brings salvation to everyone who believes'. And where does the gospel get such power if not from God himself? He does things right and puts things right – he even puts wrong people right, and he does it righteously! He is faithful to his word, so we can trust him, and by the power of the gospel, we can become like him – faithful followers of Jesus.[118]

There is nothing in the gospel that Paul could possibly be ashamed of!

Furthermore, Paul has proved himself to be 'a worker who does not need to be ashamed'[119] as a faithful steward of the mystery that had been made known to him[120] (i.e. the gospel) which he roots firmly in the Old Testament Scriptures. Towards the end of his life, he passes on the baton to Timothy, entrusting him with the responsibility to pass it on faithfully to 'reliable people who will also be qualified to teach others.' (2 Timothy 2:2) We stand in the direct line of that tradition, with the responsibility not only to receive this message, but

117 Romans 1:16
118 See Romans 1:17.
119 Cf. 2 Timothy 2:15.
120 1 Corinthians 4:1-2; cf. 2 Corinthians 4:1-6

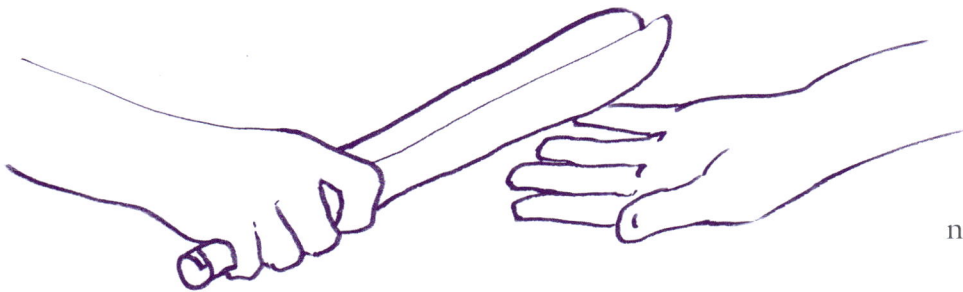

to pass it on – unchanged – to the next generation of Christian disciples. This is not achieved simply through repeating by rote, but by learning to handle the word of truth correctly.[121]

One of the best ways to do that is to self-check the message we preach against the Scriptures themselves, to adjust what we say in light of our growing knowledge of God, and to commit to an on-going process of day by day 'mind renewal',[122] welcoming the influence of the Spirit of God who transforms our thinking (and living) as we reflect on 'what is written'.

Review your 'first thoughts' about the gospel message (p.5).

Would you want to put anything differently in light of what you have discovered from God's word?

Is there anything you would now want to add as a 'core component' of the gospel?

----

121 See 2 Timothy 2:15.
122 Romans 12:2

Is there anything that you would see as being perhaps less central to the gospel than you previously thought? (If so, how might this affect the way you relate to other Christians who perhaps think a little differently from you on that point?)

Of course, in this workbook, we have only begun to explore the question: 'The gospel – what is it?' As we go on reading the Bible in the light of Jesus we shall discover more and more of 'the gospel of God'.

Some further reading

As with most subjects, there are points which equally faithful Bible readers understand differently. Because of the importance of the gospel, those differences are often expressed quite passionately. The aim of these workbooks is to help you shape your own understanding of the subject in light of Scripture, rather than to persuade you to accept the views of the workbook writer.

It is ok to disagree – as long as we are not disagreeable! None of us has perfect understanding, so as we engage with different viewpoints, we can help one another 'as iron sharpens iron' (Proverbs 27:17). If we don't simply want to spark one another off, though, I suggest the following few guidelines:

- Try to use Bible words in the same way Bible writers did, not as shorthand for something else.
- Keep your focus on what is 'of first importance' (1 Corinthians 15:3).
- Tell other people the good news of Jesus so they can be saved through faith in him.
- Go on reading the Bible and expect your appreciation of the gospel to grow.

If you would like to read some books that will further sharpen your thinking, I suggest:

Greg Gilbert, *What is the Gospel?*, Wheaton: Crossway, 2010
Scot McKnight, *The King Jesus Gospel*, Grand Rapids: Zondervan, 2011
Darrell Bock, *Recovering the Real Lost Gospel*, Nashville: B&H, 2010

If you search for those authors online you will be able to follow some of the recent debate in the U.S.

Tilsley Academy offers an on-line study module based on this workbook. I'd be glad to meet you there and to engage with your views. You can find more information at www.tilsley.academy

Look out for a forthcoming Counties publication:
Making Jesus Known Today and Tomorrow.

The Bible Project offers several free videos (and other resources) on the theme of the gospel. You may like to look here:
https://bibleproject.com/explore/video/euangelion-gospel/

THE GOSPEL – WHAT IS IT?
A Partnership Publication

Published by
Partnership, Abbey Court, Cove, Tiverton, Devon EX16 7RT

ISBN book 978 191601305 6
ISBN ebook 978 191601307 0

British Library cataloguing and data
A catalogue record of this book is available from the British Library

Design and typesetiing by Tony Cantale Graphics
Printed in the UK by Bell & Bain, Glasgow

www.partnershipuk.org

Further information on
the Partnership Workbook series can be found at
https://partnershipuk.org/workbookseriesindex

DISCOVER
MORE